HOW TO LIVE LIKE
A ROMAN
GLADIATOR

Thanks to the creative team:

Senior Editor: Alice Peebles

Designer: Lauren Woods and
collaborate agency

First published in Great Britain in 2015
by Hungry Tomato Ltd

PO Box 181

Edenbridge

Kent, TN8 9DP

Copyright © 2015 Hungry Tomato Ltd

A CIP catalogue record for this book is
available from the British Library.

ISBN 978-1-910684-21-4

Printed and bound in China

Discover more at
www.hungrytomato.com

HOW TO LIVE LIKE
A ROMAN
GLADIATOR

By Anita Ganeri

Illustrated by Mariano Epelbaum

HUNGRY
TOMATO™

Contents

Gladiator!

It's the 1st century AD, and you've travelled back in time to a village in the Roman province of Gallia (Gaul) in northern Europe. The Romans first invaded more than 100 years ago, and have been here ever since.

My name is Felix, and this village was my home until a few days ago. Some of the Gallic tribes around here were quite happy to be ruled by the Romans, but my tribe decided to pick a fight. Big mistake. We were no match for the Roman army – their soldiers are a brilliant fighting force. Needless to say, we lost the battle and many of us were taken prisoner. We're being marched off to Rome to be sold as gladiators. Things are not looking good.

WARNING!

Once captured, your fate is out of your hands. Escape is not an option, even if you actually make it to Rome – which is not guaranteed.

By the time of this story, Rome had conquered most of the lands around the Mediterranean Sea (shown here in red), and the Romans ruled over the most powerful empire in the world – worse luck.

Rome

Mediterranean Sea

Who were the Romans?

The Romans were the people who lived in the city of Rome in Italy. Rome was founded in 753 BC by twin brothers, Romulus and Remus. They had been left to die by the river but were rescued and raised by a she-wolf. They built the city on the spot where the wolf found them. At least, that's the story the Romans have always told us.

For Sale: Gladiators!

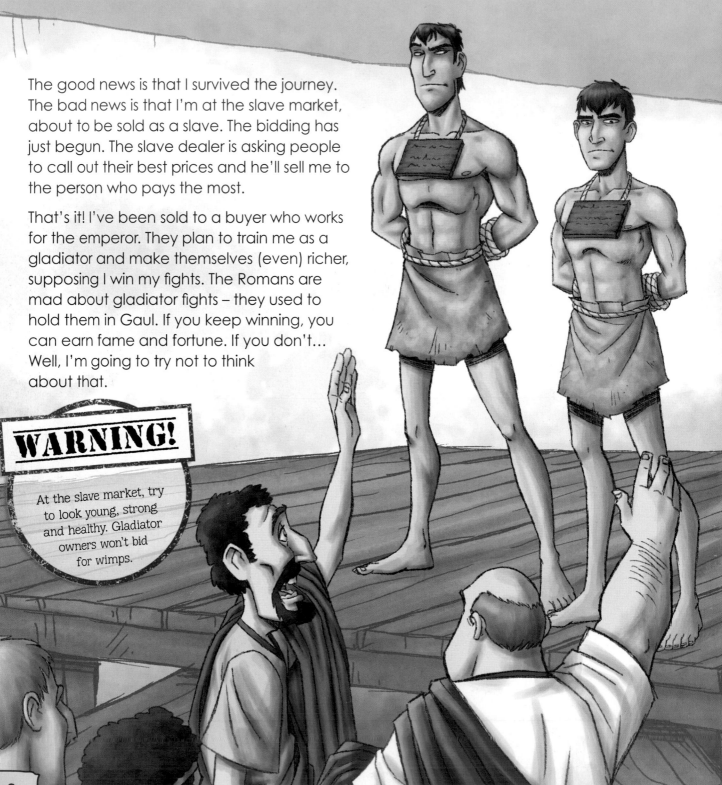

The good news is that I survived the journey. The bad news is that I'm at the slave market, about to be sold as a slave. The bidding has just begun. The slave dealer is asking people to call out their best prices and he'll sell me to the person who pays the most.

That's it! I've been sold to a buyer who works for the emperor. They plan to train me as a gladiator and make themselves (even) richer, supposing I win my fights. The Romans are mad about gladiator fights – they used to hold them in Gaul. If you keep winning, you can earn fame and fortune. If you don't... Well, I'm going to try not to think about that.

WARNING!

At the slave market, try to look young, strong and healthy. Gladiator owners won't bid for wimps.

It's a hard life being a slave in ancient Rome. You might end up labouring in a rich person's house or on a farm, or be sent down the mines or stone quarries – virtually a death sentence because they're such dangerous places to work.

Other ways of becoming a gladiator

Being taken prisoner is just one way of becoming a gladiator. You might also:

1 Be a dangerous criminal. A judge could sentence you to **crucifixion**, a stint in the slave mines or to fight as a gladiator.

2 Be a disobedient slave. Disobeying your master, or worse, threatening him with violence, will guarantee you a place at gladiator school.

3 Be in serious debt. If you owe loads of money, you may have to sell yourself to a gladiator school as a way of paying off your debts.

4 Volunteer. You can sign up as a volunteer, though it means selling yourself to a gladiator school.

Girls can also train as gladiators, though not many choose this as a career. All you need is a talent for swordfighting, and you could soon be starring in the arena as the latest novelty act.

I am Spartacus

My buyer's bought two other slaves, Marcus and Crixus, and is taking us all off to the *ludus gladiatorius* – the school where we'll be trained to fight. It'll be home for the next few months – I wonder if I'll ever see my village in Gaul again?

While our master is paying, Crixus tells us the story of Spartacus, the most famous gladiator of all. In 73 BC, Spartacus and 70 men escaped from their ludus in Capua, seizing several wagonloads of weapons and armour. They made their way to Mount Vesuvius where… But wait, I can hear our master coming back…

No one knows who the real Spartacus was. He may have come from Thrace (modern-day Bulgaria) and been taken prisoner after deserting from the Roman army.

Story of Spartacus

On Mount Vesuvius, Spartacus was joined by hundreds of other escaped slaves. For the next two years, he led his slave army – which soon numbered around 100,000 – against the Romans. By now, the Romans were seriously worried, and sent in their top generals – Lucullus, Crassus and Pompey. They defeated Spartacus and his devoted followers in battle near the port of Brindisium. It is said that Spartacus, fighting bravely, was cut down, but his body was never found.

WARNING!

If you're thinking of leading an escape from your ludus, think again – 6,000 of the rebels were crucified.

Back to School

As a gladiator, you are a valuable possession and need to prove your worth. The ludus accountant keeps tabs on how much it costs to train, feed and equip you, and balances that against how much you're likely to earn for appearing in a show.

Well, we've reached the ludus, located in another part of Rome. Luckily, our master works for the emperor so we're going to the *ludus imperialis* (the **imperial** emperor's school). It's the best there is, apparently. If we do well, we may even fight in the Colosseum – not sure if that's good or bad news.

Our master hands us over to the **lanista**, Brutus. He's the chief trainer, and does he live up to his name! He used to be a gladiator he knows all the tricks of the trade, and his job is to knock us new recruits into shape. He's also in charge of punishments, so he's the last person you'd want to mess with around here.

Who's who in the ludus

Time to meet the ludus staff who'll be looking after you during your stay. Trainee gladiators soon learn their place – right at the bottom of the pile!

Owner: the Roman who owns the gladiators and pays for their training

Lanista: directs all your training; the person you most want to impress

Armourer: keeps your armour in good condition and does running repairs

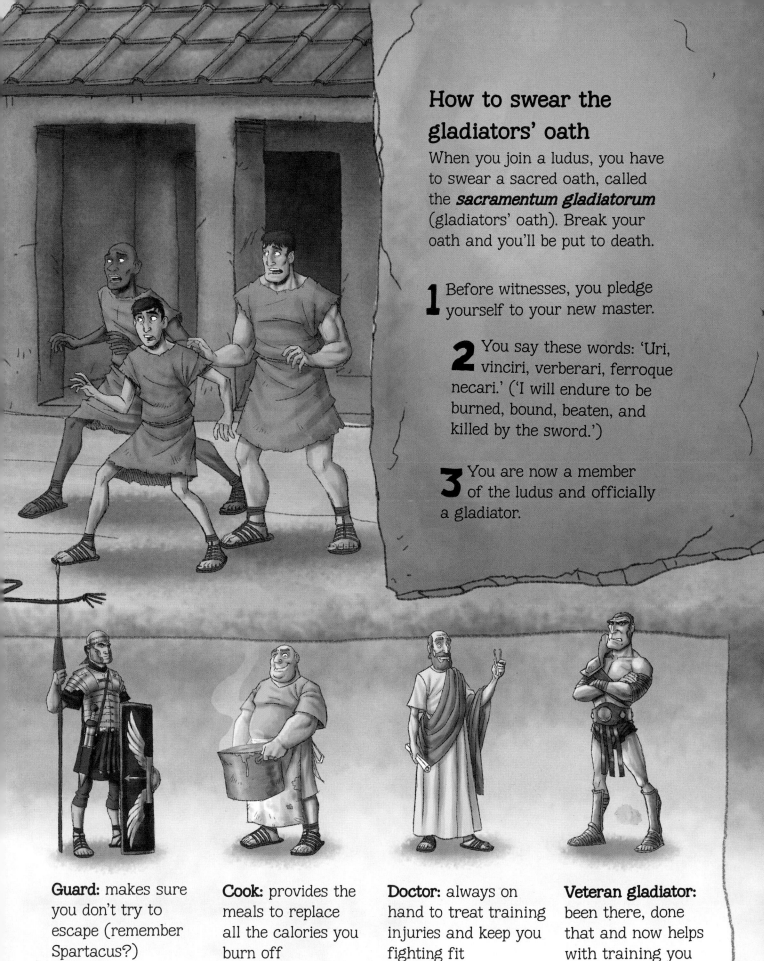

How to swear the gladiators' oath

When you join a ludus, you have to swear a sacred oath, called the *sacramentum gladiatorum* (gladiators' oath). Break your oath and you'll be put to death.

1 Before witnesses, you pledge yourself to your new master.

2 You say these words: 'Uri, vinciri, verberari, ferroque necari.' ('I will endure to be burned, bound, beaten, and killed by the sword.')

3 You are now a member of the ludus and officially a gladiator.

Guard: makes sure you don't try to escape (remember Spartacus?)

Cook: provides the meals to replace all the calories you burn off

Doctor: always on hand to treat training injuries and keep you fighting fit

Veteran gladiator: been there, done that and now helps with training you

13

Gladiator in Training

Our first day of training is over and I'm so tired, I can hardly move. And it's the same again tomorrow, and the next day, and the next...To practise swordfighting, we spent hours hacking away at the **palus** — it's a wooden post stuck in the ground. The idea is to practise the essential blocking and cutting moves we'll need in a real fight.

But they don't give us real swords – apparently, they don't trust us enough. Instead, we use wooden swords, so I've got blisters and splinters, not to mention aches and pains. Think I'll head off for a massage before dinner time.

How to choose a gladiator name

If you're going to make a splash in the arena, you'll need a new name to fight under.

1 Pick a name from one of the great heroes of mythology, such as Hector or Ajax.

2 Or choose one with a meaning, such as Felix ('Happy') or Maximus ('Greatest').

Punishments

If you don't train hard enough, you'll be whipped to teach you a lesson. And don't even think about trying to escape. If you're caught, you might be branded as a runaway slave, flogged (even more) or thrown into the rat-infested ludus prison.

Training also helps build up your muscles; brute strength is highly prized in a gladiator. When you're not at the palus, you'll be lifting heavy weights.

The Heavy Mob

The time has come for the lanista to decide which type of gladiator we're each going to be. He says he's basing his decision on whether we're big and brawny, or small and fast on our feet. Here he comes…

Well, Marcus is a *retiarius* and Crixus is a Thracian. I'm going to be a *murmillo* or 'fish man'. We're all getting different types of armour and weapons. Mine's a short sword and a big, rectangular shield, with a full-face helmet. The helmet's got a crest that looks like a fish's fin (can't see it myself). A murmillo usually fights against Thracians, so I guess it's me against Crixus from now on.

Which type of gladiator are you?

1 PROVOCATOR Heavyweight expert at close-contact fighting; usual opponents are other provocators

2 THRACIAN Armed with short sword and small shield; wears long shin guards and a feathered helmet

3 MURMILLO Wears a full-face helmet with a fin-like crest; fights against Thracians

4 RETIARIUS The 'net man' who fights with a net and trident, his left arm heavily bandaged for protection

5 SECUTOR Chases a retiarius; wears a smooth, egg-shaped helmet that a net cannot get caught on

6 SANDABATUS Only fights another sandabatus; wears a helmet without eyeholes so cannot see his opponent

Being small and light can be an advantage for a gladiator. You can skip around the heavyweights and aren't slowed down by cumbersome armour.

5

6

3

4

WARNING!

Sometimes the lanista asks trainees which sort of gladiator they want to be. And sometimes he doesn't...

If you're good with horses, you might become an *essedarius*: a gladiator who drives a horse-drawn chariot. You charge at your opponent, aimimg to run them over or stab them with your spear.

Ludus Life

WARNING!

Try not to flinch or show pain when the doctor is treating you. Ouch!

It costs an owner a fortune to buy, train and equip a gladiator, so he needs to make sure we're looked after well. There's no point in us dying before we even get to the arena – he wouldn't get his money back. This means making sure we're properly fed, get plenty of exercise and have the best possible medical care.

After a hard day's training, we head back to our **barracks** for dinner. We're always starving, but luckily, there's always plenty to eat. It's not as tasty as the food my Mum used to cook at home but it's good for us, so we keep being told.

If you are injured in training, you can expect skilled medical care. The ludus doctor will dress your wounds and have you ready for the next bout in no time at all. Some doctors achieve great things. One of the top docs in the Roman world, Galen, began by treating gladiators and went on to become the emperor's private physician.

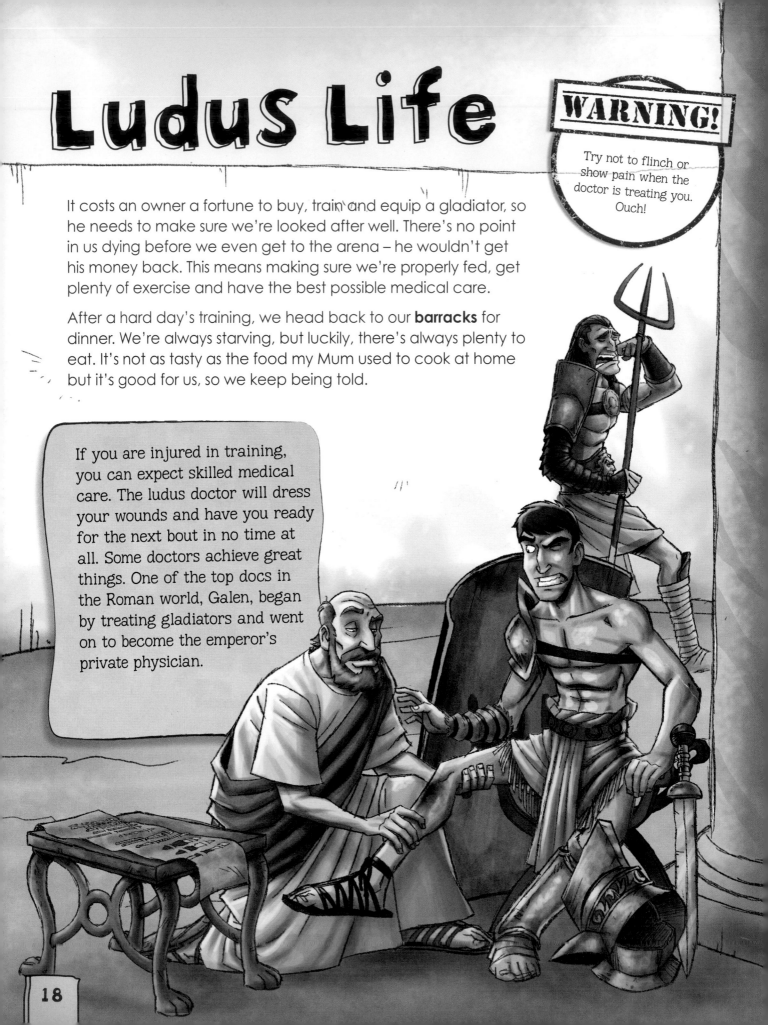

Some gladiators trained in the ludus but did not live there. Wealthy Romans kept them as bodyguards or to put on a show at the end of a dinner party.

On the menu

Want to eat like a gladiator?
Here's what's on the menu:

1 Barley: the staple part of your diet. You'll be eating this at every meal. (Note: barley is really animal food – a sign of your low status!)

2 Beans and dried fruit: like everybody else, gladiators need their five fruit and veg a day.

3 Meat: your diet is mainly vegetarian but you might be given the odd tiger steak.

4 Energy drink: meals are washed down with a mixture of vinegar, crushed animal bones and ash, to give you energy and strengthen your bones.

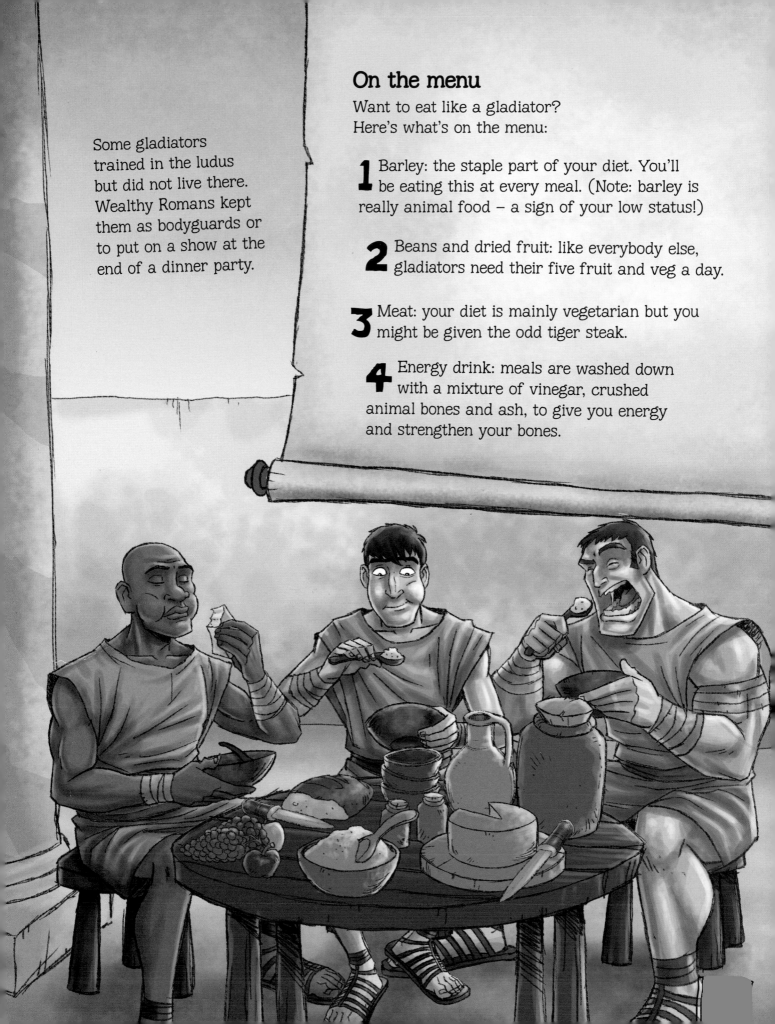

The Big Day Arrives

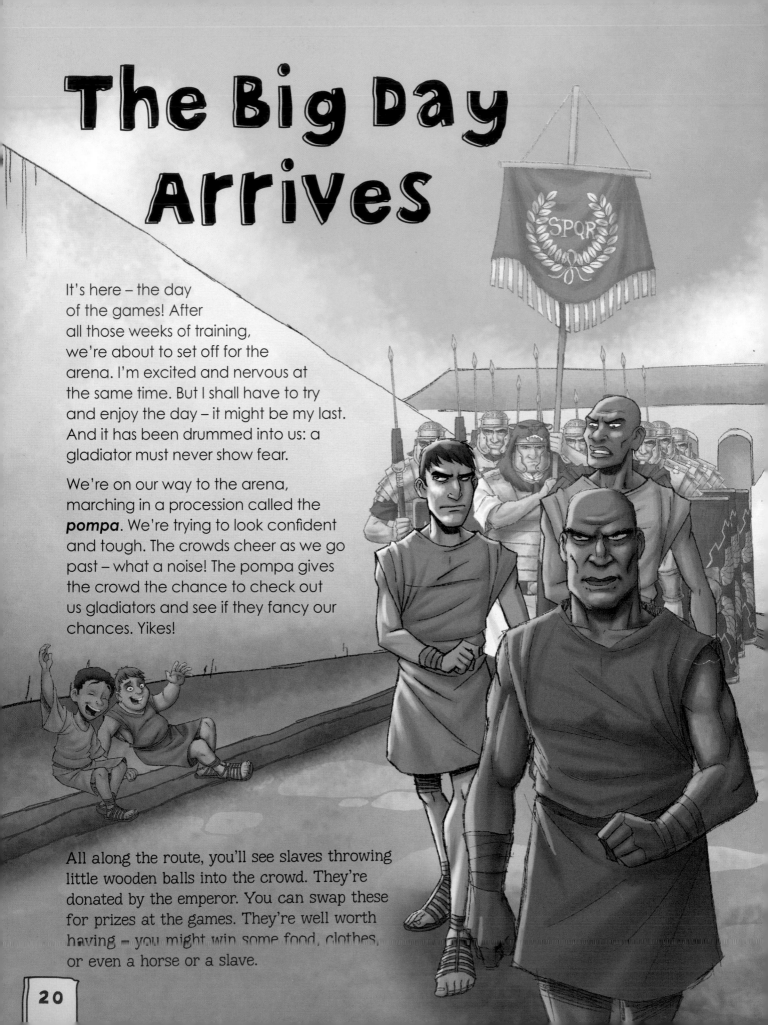

It's here – the day of the games! After all those weeks of training, we're about to set off for the arena. I'm excited and nervous at the same time. But I shall have to try and enjoy the day – it might be my last. And it has been drummed into us: a gladiator must never show fear.

We're on our way to the arena, marching in a procession called the *pompa*. We're trying to look confident and tough. The crowds cheer as we go past – what a noise! The pompa gives the crowd the chance to check out us gladiators and see if they fancy our chances. Yikes!

All along the route, you'll see slaves throwing little wooden balls into the crowd. They're donated by the emperor. You can swap these for prizes at the games. They're well worth having – you might win some food, clothes, or even a horse or a slave.

The organizers want a good turn-out, so they've been advertising the games for days, with street criers calling out the names of the gladiators, notices painted on walls and posters in the market place.

How to eat (and possibly enjoy) your last meal

The night before the games, you'll have a splendid feast – in case it's your last meal. Try not to overeat – your digestive system's not used to such rich food. Members of the public can come and watch you eat, and perhaps take a last message to your family.

Inside the Arena

We've reached the arena, where we're announced to the crowd. We stop in front of the emperor's box and raise our right arms to salute him. Then we call out to him, 'Ave, Caesar! Morituri te salutamus!' ('Hail, Caesar! We who are about to die salute you!') I need to hold my nerve. I just wish my knees would stop knocking.

Before we go off for a last bit of light training (we're not on until the afternoon), I'm taking the chance to have a quick glance round. The **Colosseum** is overwhelming, and it's packed with spectators – around 50,000, I've heard. Wish my family could see me now (or not) – they'd be so proud (or not).

The floor of the Colosseum is wooden and covered in sand. Underneath is a complex of tunnels, passages and cages where gladiators and wild animals are kept. The gladiators' barracks at the imperial ludus are connected to the arena by tunnels.

How to grab the best seat

The seats in the Colosseum are arranged in **tiers**. Wealthy Romans sit lower down where they have a really good view; poor people sit higher up and slaves right at the back. The best seats are in the emperor's box at the north end of the arena.

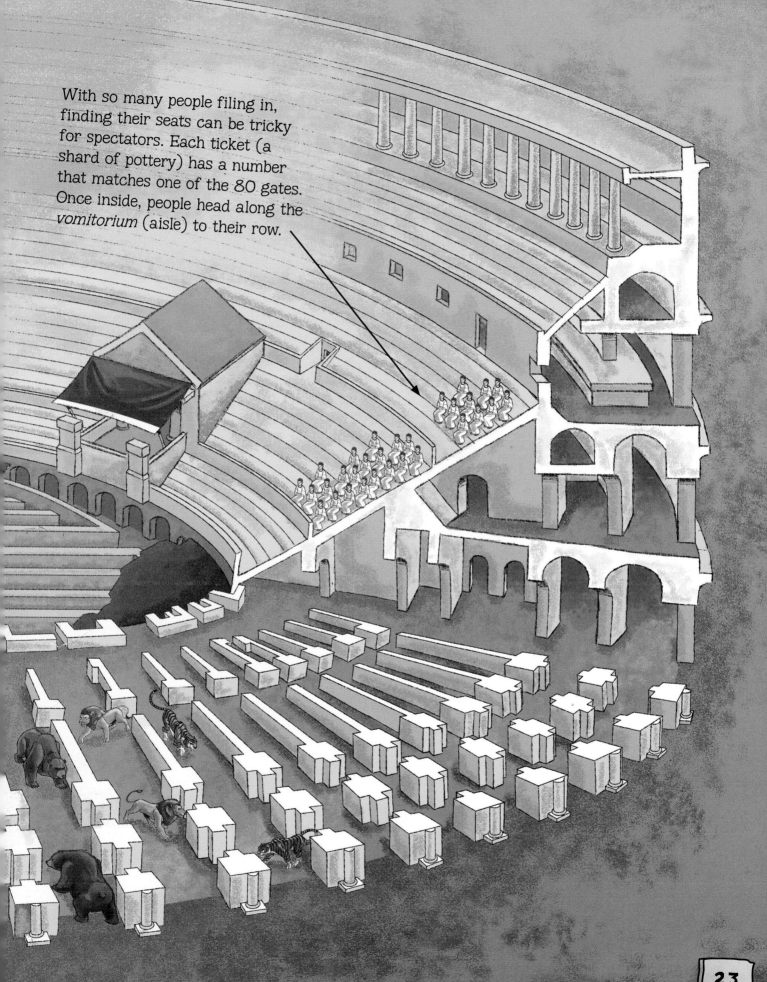

With so many people filing in, finding their seats can be tricky for spectators. Each ticket (a shard of pottery) has a number that matches one of the 80 gates. Once inside, people head along the *vomitorium* (aisle) to their row.

Thrown to the Lions

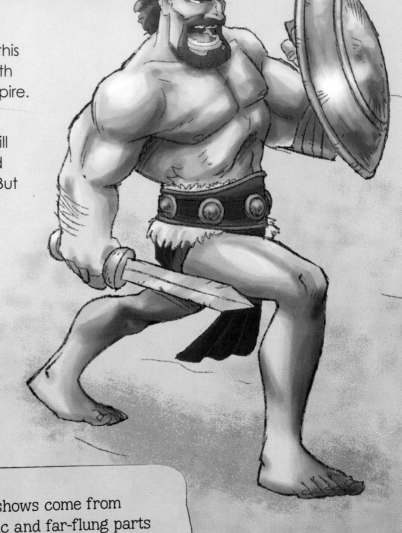

The games are about to begin, and this morning there's a wild beast hunt, with animals brought from all over the Empire.

The hunter's called a *bestiarius*. Sometimes he's specially trained to kill animals, and is armed with a net and spear. He usually comes out on top. But sometimes he's an unarmed criminal who's thrown to the lions as his punishment. He doesn't stand a chance, but by that time half of the spectators have gone for lunch.

The wild beasts used in the shows come from Africa and many other exotic and far-flung parts of the Roman world. They include lions, which are guaranteed crowd-pleasers , leopards, elephants, giraffes and bears. So many animals are needed for the shows that some have been hunted almost to the point of extinction.

Any animals killed are quickly turned into meat and sold off. In the days following the games, butchers' shops stock a tasty range of giraffe, hippopotamus and elephant steaks, and wealthy Romans (who will eat almost anything) are happy to tuck in.

WARNING!

You'll need to keep your wits about you – these animals are seriously wild, so are sure to lash out in the crazy atmosphere of the arena.

Let the Bout Begin!

After lunch, I'm on second, so I've been warming up behind the scenes. A huge roar has gone up from the crowd, which can only mean one thing… the first bout has finished and it's my turn next.

I am drawn against a Thracian who puts up a pretty good fight. For a while, it looks as if he is going to win but I remember my training and fight back hard. Then I have a stroke of luck – badly injured, he trips and falls. As I lift my sword for the final blow, the crowd begin shouting, 'Habet! Hoc habet!' ('Got him! He's had it!') He lies on the ground, then slowly raises his finger…

WARNING!

Don't stop fighting. If you do, a slave may prod you with a red-hot iron.

In case you die in the arena, your lanista has already set a price on your life. If you don't make it, this is the amount the games' organizer has to pay out. The going rate's around 3,000 **sestertii** for a first-timer to 15,000 sestertii for a top-notch star.

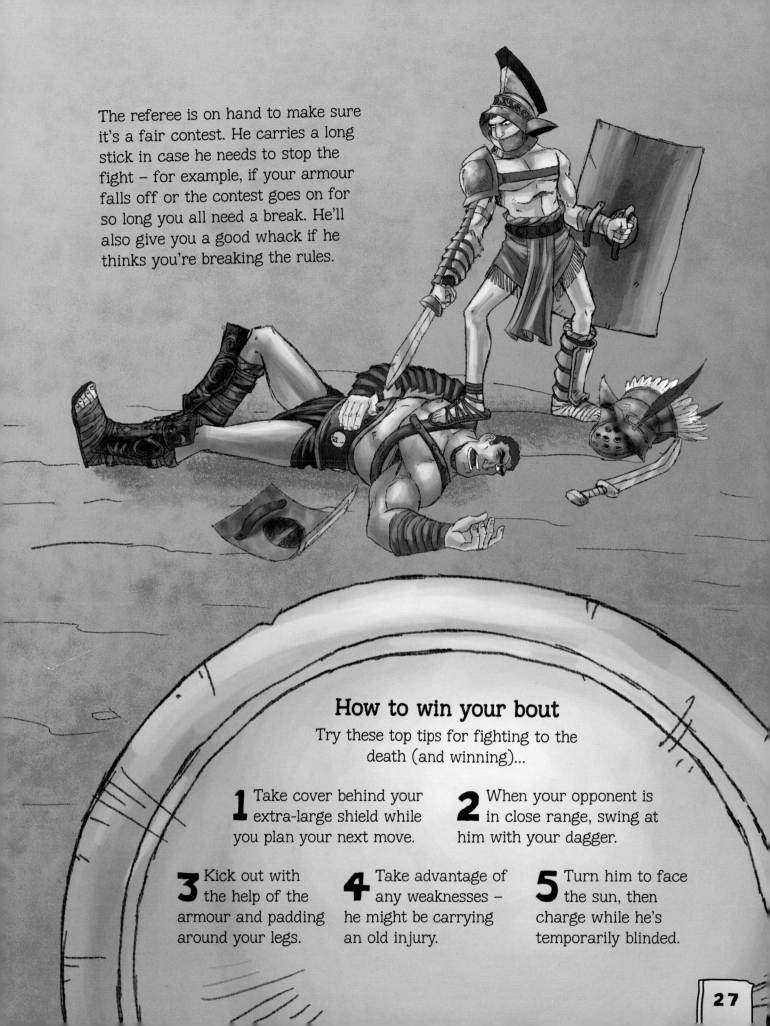

The referee is on hand to make sure it's a fair contest. He carries a long stick in case he needs to stop the fight – for example, if your armour falls off or the contest goes on for so long you all need a break. He'll also give you a good whack if he thinks you're breaking the rules.

How to win your bout

Try these top tips for fighting to the death (and winning)...

1 Take cover behind your extra-large shield while you plan your next move.

2 When your opponent is in close range, swing at him with your dagger.

3 Kick out with the help of the armour and padding around your legs.

4 Take advantage of any weaknesses – he might be carrying an old injury.

5 Turn him to face the sun, then charge while he's temporarily blinded.

Dead or Alive?

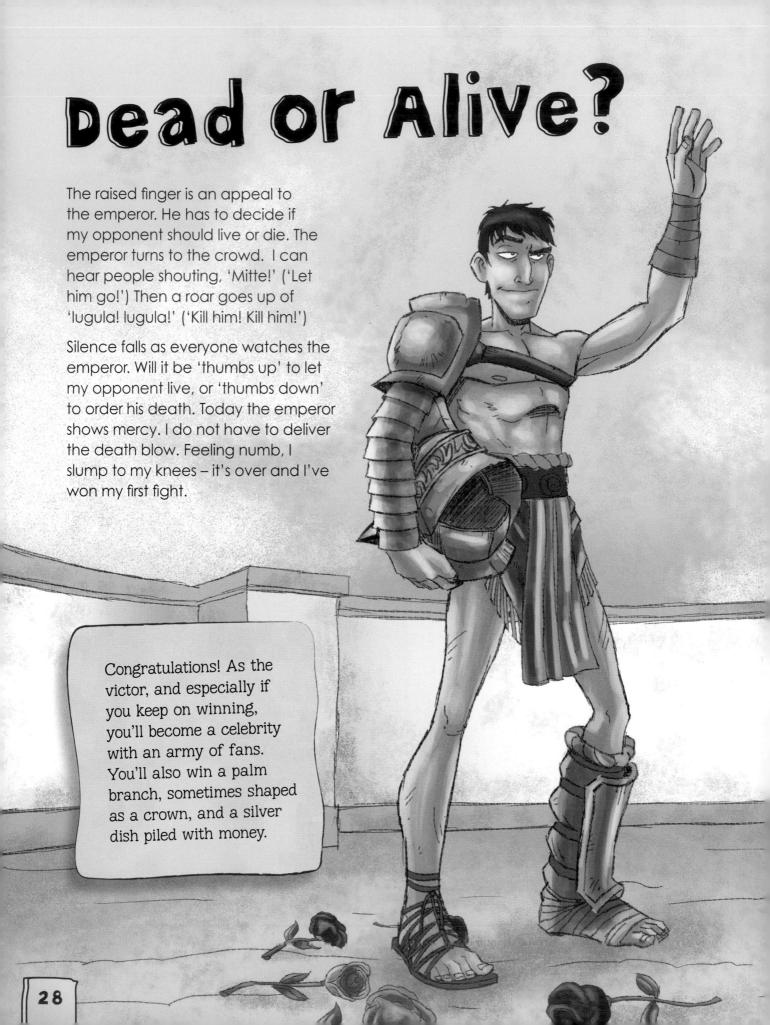

The raised finger is an appeal to the emperor. He has to decide if my opponent should live or die. The emperor turns to the crowd. I can hear people shouting, 'Mitte!' ('Let him go!') Then a roar goes up of 'lugula! lugula!' ('Kill him! Kill him!')

Silence falls as everyone watches the emperor. Will it be 'thumbs up' to let my opponent live, or 'thumbs down' to order his death. Today the emperor shows mercy. I do not have to deliver the death blow. Feeling numb, I slump to my knees – it's over and I've won my first fight.

Congratulations! As the victor, and especially if you keep on winning, you'll become a celebrity with an army of fans. You'll also win a palm branch, sometimes shaped as a crown, and a silver dish piled with money.

If you continue to win (and there are no guarantees), you may be presented with a *rudis* (wooden sword). This marks the end of your service and the start of your freedom. You could go back home to your family, or find work as a trainer at a gladiator school.

WARNING!

Winning has its downside. It means you live to fight another day.

If a gladiator dies, his body is dragged from the arena, and fresh sand sprinkled over the blood. To make sure he isn't just pretending, one man dressed as Charun (who guards the Underworld) hits him with his hammer, while another, dressed as Mercury (messenger of the gods) pokes him with a red-hot stick.

Ten gory gladiator facts

1 The word 'gladiator' comes from the Latin *gladius*, the sword wielded by foot soldiers

2 The first gladiator fight probably took place at a funeral, in honour of the dead man.

3 A gladiator's life was often brutal and short. Most only lived to their mid-20s, at most.

4 If the emperor decided a wounded gladiator should die, the victor stabbed his opponent through the neck.

5 During the 100-day opening games at the Colosseum, around 9,000 animals were killed.

6 Before the real combat began, there was a mock fight between two retired fighters armed with wooden swords.

7 Several Roman emperors took part in gladiator fights, and guess what? They always won.

8 Roman children played with gladiator action figures made from clay – gladiators were superstars!

9 Dead gladiators were dragged through the Porta Libitinensis (Gate of Death), where their bodies were stripped and their weapons given back to their lanista.

10 Gladiators belonged to special burial clubs that made sure they would receive a decent funeral.

Glossary

Barracks

Blocks of accommodation for soldiers, or in this case, gladiators

Colosseum

The largest amphitheatre (open-air venue) in the Roman Empire

Crucifixion

A form of punishment in which the victim was nailed to a wooden cross

Imperial

Connected to the emperor or the empire

Lanista

The manager and chief trainer of a gladiator school

Ludus gladiatorius

A school where gladiators lived and trained

Palus

A wooden post used by gladiators for practising swordfighting skills

Pompa

The procession of the gladiators into the arena at the start of the games

Sacramentum gladiatorum

The sacred oath sworn by gladiators as they began their training

Sestertii

Ancient Roman coins made from brass

Tiers

Rows of seats, placed one above the other

INDEX

The Author
Anita Ganeri is an award-winning author of educational children's books. She has written on a huge variety of subjects, from Vikings to viruses and from Romans to world religions. She was born in India but now lives in England with her family and pets.

The Artist
Mariano Epelbaum was born in Buenos Aires, Argentina. He grew up drawing and looking at small insects under the stones in the garden of his grandmother's house. He has worked as an art director and character designer for many films in Argentina and Spain.